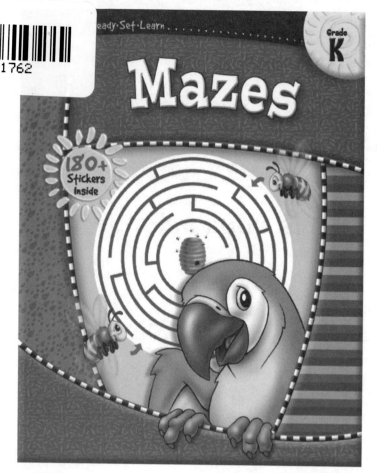

Ready·Set·Learn

Mazes

Grade **K**

180+ Stickers Inside

Managing Editor
Ina Massler Levin, M.A.

Editor
Eric Migliaccio

Contributing Editor
Sarah Smith

Creative Director
Karen J. Goldfluss, M.S. Ed.

Cover Design
Tony Carrillo / Marilyn Goldberg

Teacher Created Resources, Inc.
12621 Western Avenue
Garden Grove, CA 92841
www.teachercreated.com

ISBN: 978-1-4206-5962-7

©2007 Teacher Created Resources, Inc.
Reprinted, 2017 (PO600799)
Made in U.S.A.

Teacher Created Resources

This book belongs to

_____

Ready·Set·Learn

2

Get Ready to Learn!

Get ready, get set, and go! Boost your child's learning with this exciting series of books. Geared to help children practice and master many needed skills, the Ready·Set·Learn books are bursting with 64 pages of learning fun. Use these books for . . .

※ enrichment   ※ skills reinforcement   ※ extra practice

With their smaller size, the Ready·Set·Learn books fit easily in children's hands, backpacks, and book bags. All your child needs to get started are pencils, crayons, and colored pencils.

A full sheet of colorful stickers is included. Use these stickers for . . .

※ decorating pages

※ rewarding outstanding effort

※ keeping track of completed pages

Celebrate your child's progress by using these stickers on the reward chart located on the inside cover. The blue-ribbon sticker fits perfectly on the certificate on page 64.

With Ready·Set·Learn and a little encouragement, your child will be on the fast track to learning fun!

Peter's Ride

4

Mary's Little Lamb

SCHOOL

Head for Home

6

Time to Change

Eggs

8

Where Is My Teddy?

Look Who Hatched

10

Fetch a Pail of Water

Time to Travel

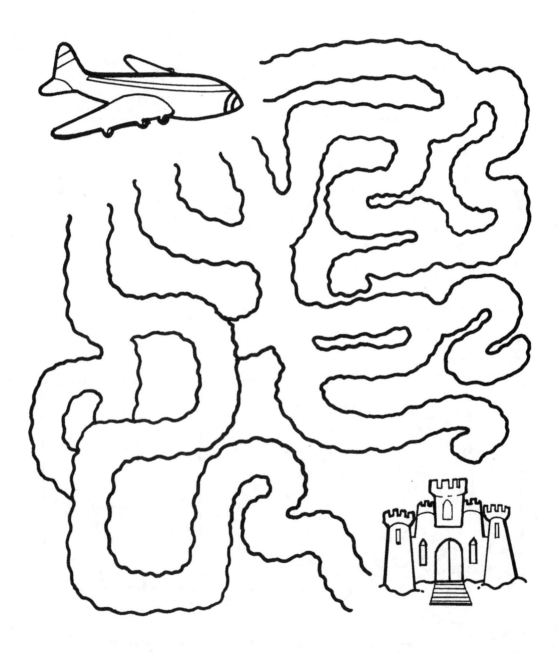

Snake Slithers Home

#5962 Mazes

Grandma's House

14

Find the School

Where Is My Mother?

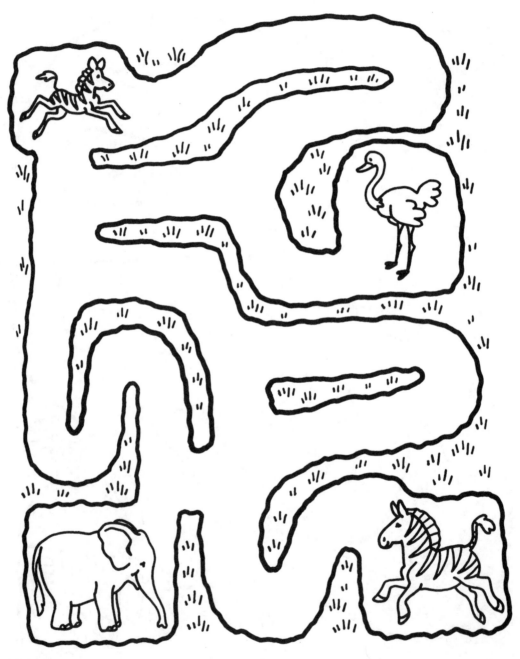

Time to Play

A Dog Goes to School

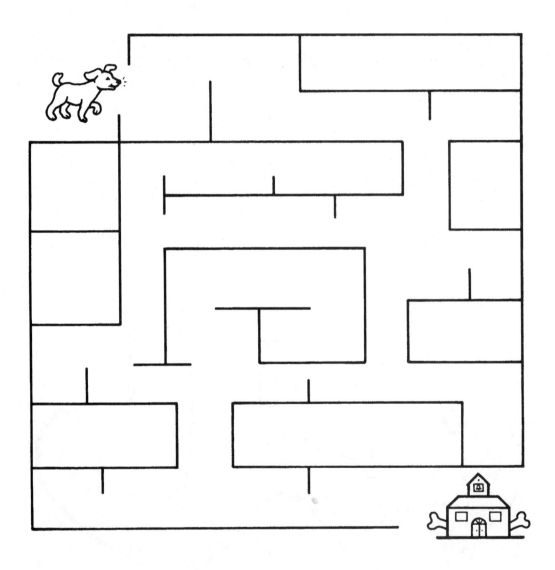

18

Find the Nest

Meow!

20

Trick or Treat

Hibernation

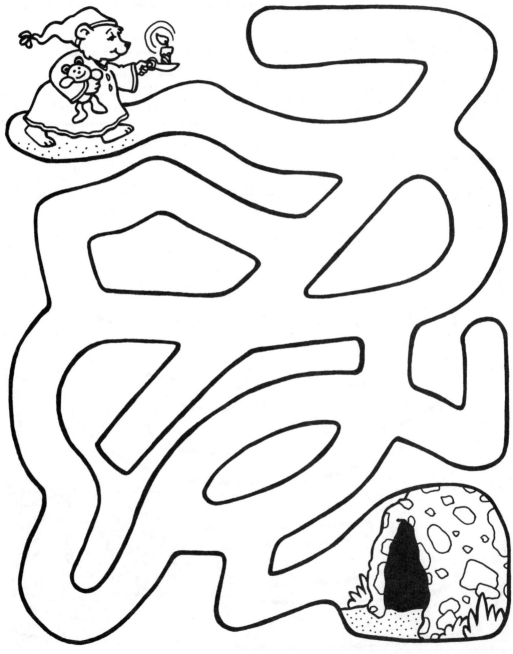

Which Path?

Pears for Panda

24

Lost

25

House Key

Help the Cow

To the Firehouse

Where Is My Pony?

Where Is Our Barn?

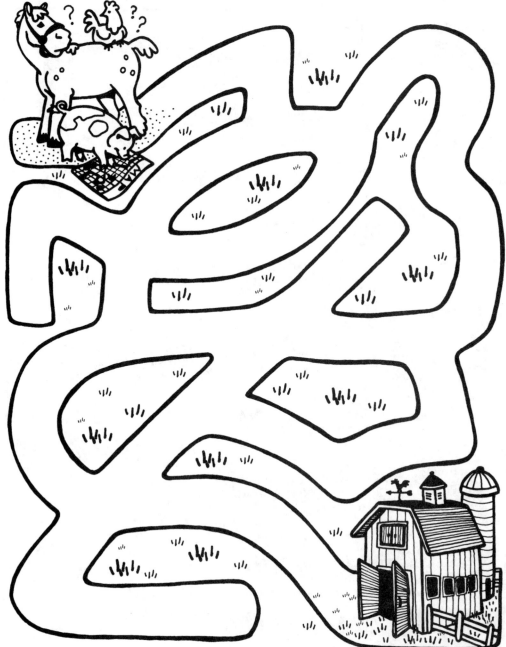

Winter Is Here!

Honey Tastes Good

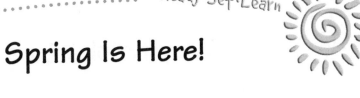

Spring Is Here!

Which Way to the Castle?

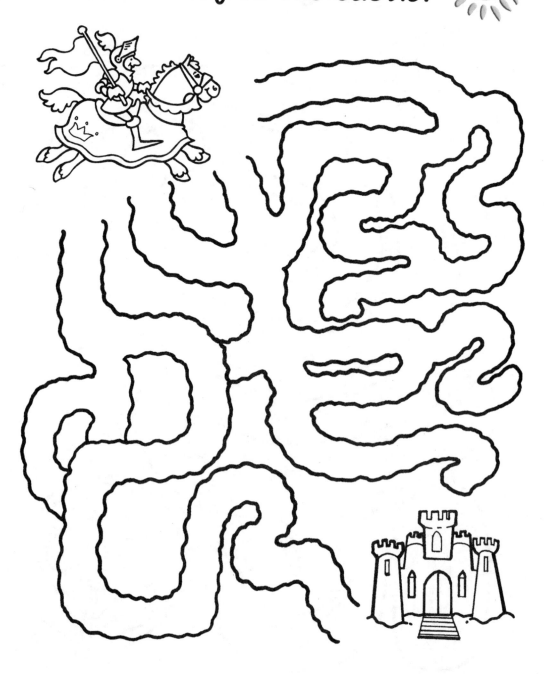

34

Polish the Bell

Get Through the Garden

Wake Up Time

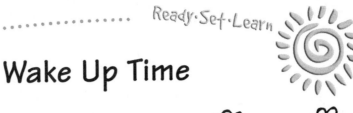

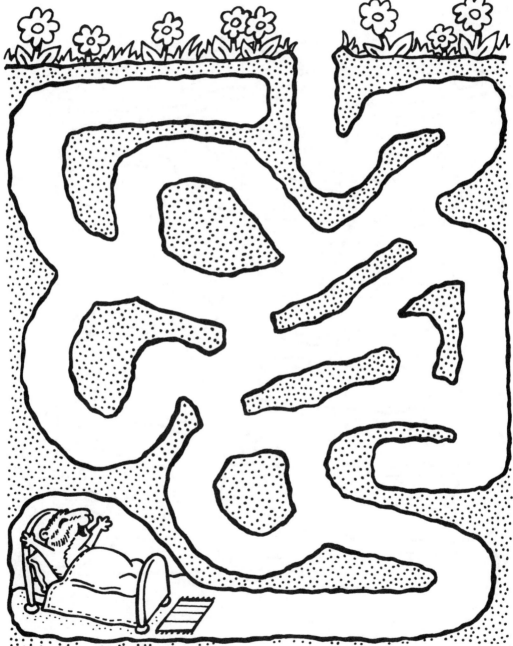

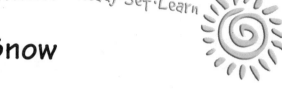
Snow

The Path to School

Flowers for Mom

A Gift for Dad

A Gathering of Friends

Feeding Time

Amy's Lost Bear

44

Find the Ballerina

Where Is Home?

Fall Leaves

Polar Bear Maze

Hansel and Gretel

The Circus

To the Lake We Go

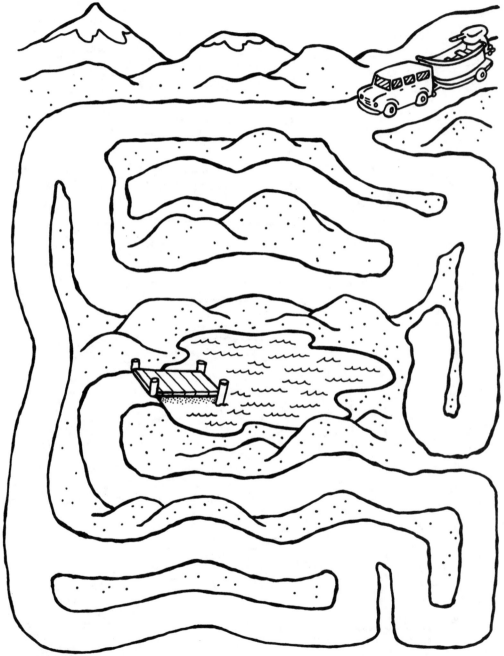

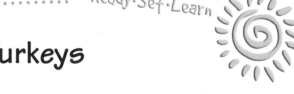

Turkeys

52

The Lion and the Lollipop

Cheese Please

Race to the Pond

Mushroom Maze

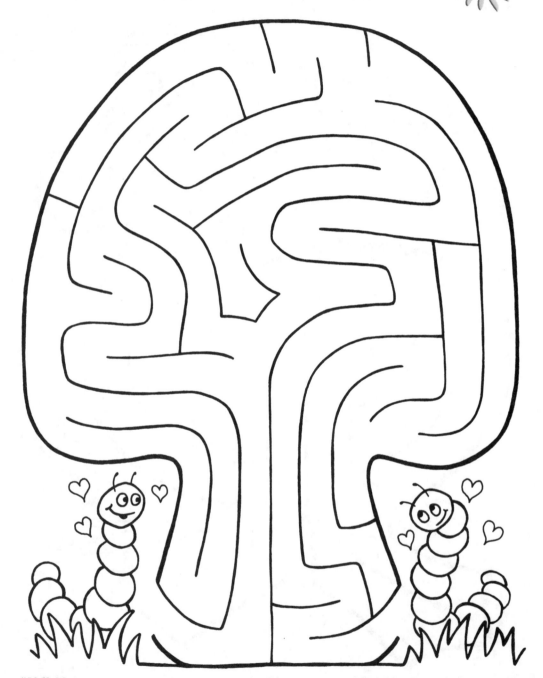

Play That Fiddle!

It's Amazing!

58

Palm Paradise

Puppy Food

60

Cookie Jar Maze

What's for Dessert?

This Award
Is Presented To

_____

for

★ Doing Your Best

★ Trying Hard

★ Not Giving Up

★ Making a
  Great Effort

64